Anonymous

**Hillside rhymes**

Anonymous

**Hillside rhymes**

ISBN/EAN: 9783337261764

Printed in Europe, USA, Canada, Australia, Japan

Cover: Foto ©Thomas Meinert / pixelio.de

More available books at **www.hansebooks.com**

# HILLSIDE RHYMES.

PUBLISHED BY

# JAMES MACLEHOSE, GLASGOW.

———

*MACMILLAN AND CO., LONDON.*

| | | |
|---|---|---|
| *Edinburgh,* | . . | *Edmonston & Douglas.* |
| *Dublin,* | . . . | *W. H. Smith & Son.* |

———

MDCCCLXXII.

# HILLSIDE RHYMES

AMONG THE ROCKS HE WENT
AND STILL LOOKED UP TO SUN AND CLOUD
AND LISTENED TO THE WIND

Glasgow
JAMES MACLEHOSE
PUBLISHER TO THE UNIVERSITY

LONDON : MACMILLAN AND CO.
1872

PRINTED BY ROBERT MACLEHOSE.

# CONTENTS.

# HILLSIDE RHYMES.

## THE GREY STONE ON DOLLAR
## LAW

Aye there it stands, the old grey stone,
  Full five feet high above the ground,
Right in the middle of the track,
  The benty track that winds around

The Hill of Grief, vast, broad, and high;
  It stands before the west'ring sun,
It looks across the farthest hills,
  It hears the sough of burns far down.

No scroll or name the lone stone bears,
A slab of whinstone, weather-grey,
Wearing the same sad quiet face
In summer sun and winter day.

Short grass and mosses round it creep,
Show a scant green at summer tide;
No care it has for present life,
The stone and shadow by its side.

What memory wert thou meant to keep,
Thou grey, grim thing of other years?
Stand'st thou the speechless symbol here
Of Faith or Hope, of Love or Tears?

In the far mists of early time,
Did heart deep stirr'd by pious fear,
Seeking its God on solemn height,
In darkling Faith thee heavenward rear?

Did native Briton mourn his chief.

  And lay him on this lonely height.

To list the voices of his sires,

  In the weird gusty winds o' night?


Or dost thou mark the sacred spot,

  Where Merlin fell, the poet-seer,

As on the mountain solitudes

  He flitted past, a form of tear?


Ah! well he lov'd the Powsail Burn,

  Ah! well he lov'd the Powsail Glen :

And there beside his fountain clear,

  He sooth'd the frenzy of his brain.


The wayward music of the stream

  Found echo in the poet's heart :

The fitful pulses of the burn,

  As broken rhythm of his art,

Ah, Merlin! restless was thy life,
    As the bold stream whose circles sweep
Mid rocky boulders to its close,
    By thy lone grave, in calm so deep,—

In calm so deep, where placid Tweed,
    Stills the rude stream that to it flows;
And hushes all its rushing tide,
    In longing for thy sweet repose.

For no one ever lov'd the Tweed,
    Who was not lov'd by it in turn;
It smil'd in gentle Merlin's face,
    It soughs in sorrow round his bourn.

Or mark'st thou where, on darksome night,
    In fierce Hot Trod, with panting breath,
Men press'd the reiver in his track,
    And left him done to bloody death?

When flam'd the straw-wisp on the spear.
  Swift up the Hope with flick'ring flare,
Keen faces following in its wake,
  Rock, pool, and stream in ruddy glare.


It mov'd a guiding light to death,
  It mov'd a gleaming thing of air;
And where the deed of blood was done,
  As life went out, quench'd straightway there.


Stone! In the sight of all the hills,
  Here looking to the western sun,
Amid the sough of all the burns,
  Thy secret wilt thou tell to none.


Thou bear'st the one sad, quiet face,
  Let Summer woo or Winter rave;
Thy root unseen rests in the moor,
  Thy story in the silent grave.

## THE PRIMROSE

Closely does the Primrose nestle,
   Nestle 'neath the budding tree,
Overhead the leafless branches,
   Fain, pale flower, to shelter thee.

Op'ning on the sight 'mid bleakness,
   While rude winds their stay prolong;
When the Summer comes in beauty.
   Loit'ring still the woods among.

With a modest grace so winning,
   Lifting, with a look of love,
Thy large eyes so soft and dewy
   To the pure light from above.

Sparkle on thy green leaves, gem-like,

Pearly rain-drops, softly clear,

Gently shed from heaven upon thee,

Best lov'd of the youthful year.


Holiest spot of all the woodland

Is thy shelter'd, shady place,

Happiest in thy quiet smile, and

In the blessing of thy face.

## SPRING—A REMINISCENCE

In days of Spring, now long ago, that rise
In holy light upon the memory,
'Mid sunny glints on morns of April days,
Soft winds at noon, spring notes of happy birds,
And buds upon the trees, and all the greenness
Of the early grass,—O well do I recall
The first fresh feelings of the heart that filled
At sight of crocus and of snowdrop fair
On sunny bank that slop'd to the clear stream;
And how, a wond'ring child, I stood subdued
By the new beauty which I would not harm,
Feeling it sacred as the life of God.
And now, on looking back, nothing stands out,
In a long lapse of time, save that green bank,
Whereon the circles of the years were told
By the return of those sweet lowly flowers.

## THE LAIRD'S TRYST

" Ye'll no gang wi' the Laird the nicht, Ailie,
    Ye'll no gang wi' the Laird the nicht;
He's o'er grand a lad for you, Ailie,
    And maybe ye're no daeing richt."

" I'll gang wi' the Laird the nicht, John,
    I'll gang wi' the Laird the nicht;
He's mair to me than ony, John,
    He's mair to me than the richt."

"'There is nae moon the nicht, Ailie,
    There is nae moon the nicht;
There are weird sounds i' the Hope, Ailie,
    And moanings i' the Hicht.

" It's a dreary darksome Stell, Ailie,
  It's a dreary darksome Stell;
And the burn soughs eerie by, Ailie,
  And there's naebody there to tell."


" Dinna try to frichten me, John,
  Dinna try to frichten me;
Ye want me for yersel', John,
  But I wot it canna be.


" What care I for a' it's eerie, John,
  What care I for a' it's eerie?
When the Laird's there himsel', John,
  Fond love will mak it cheerie."


" Sin' the sweet Simmer time, Ailie,
  Sin' the sweet Simmer time;
Ye're heart has changed frae me, Ailie;
  May God forgive his crime.

" It's a dreary darksome Stell, Ailie.

 It's a dreary darksome Stell;

And there's a new howkit grave, Ailie,

 For your unborn bairn and yoursel'.


" 'Tween the rude stroke and the fa', Ailie,

 'Tween the rude stroke and the fa';

God's grace licht on your face, Ailie,

 On your face ere ye pass awa'."

## THE LAIRD'S GRAVE

Lang years have gane sin' trystin' time,
　The Laird's locks now are thin and gray,
At Kirk or Market he has been
　Never once sin' the trystin' day.


By himsel' he daunders on the hill,
　Aye seeing, in the gloamin' lone,
The vision of a pale young face,
　And hearing aye a piteous moan.


In thick o' the Stell they found him deid,
　Deid hangin' on the trystin' tree,
Aye haunted by the pale fair face,
　Weary of the weird he had to dree.

They yirded him in unhallow'd ground,
   The Laird that made awa' wi' himsel':
In a hole beneath the dark fir boughs,
   In the far, deep shade of the dreary Stell.


A mound above him fenc'd by fear,
   Not once ev'n ting'd by green of Spring.
Or lit by smile of Summer sun,
   No blessing comes to the eerie thing.


He smoor'd the young life i' the red earth,
   The red earth now lies him abune :
And ne'er a finger o' heaven will touch't,
   Save shudd'ring glint o' the hast'ning mune.


And then o' nights no wind doun the glen
   That does not stay, and sough, and rave,
'Mid the wearied firs o' the gloomy Stell,
   In whose heart lies the unhallow'd grave.

## MOORBURN IN SPRING

Oft on a dusky night of March, I've watch'd
The hills a-glow with moorburn,—crescent lines
Of fiery tongues, leaping along, and fast
Up-licking in their round the crackling heath;—
Aye snatching impulse from the facing wind,
Wav'ring, inconstant, and yet pressing on
Fatefully, as a spirit that, conscious
Of its fierce strength, plays free with its resolve,
Yet in the end fails not to gain its goal.
The glowing circle moves, a heart of fire,
Gleaming amid the dim and trailing smoke,
That falls and rises on the fitful air.

Sometimes far east, above the umber'd hills,

The moon would rise, large-orb'd, and steadily,

In silent power of heavenly influence,

Subdue the shifting, chequer'd scene of earth,

To perfect oneness with her own clear beauty.

Then I would long, with bounding heart, to be

Away among the fiery-crested hills,

Or wander 'mid the deep'nings of the glens.

## THE WEIRD OF DAWYCK

Old Dawyck was late late on the hill,
  The gloamin' shade came slowly down,
O'er crescent brow of massive Scrape,
  Where red scaurs cleave the heather brown.

The Peel had stood 'mid its old wood
  Enfolded by its guardian hill,
Now bright in gleam, now deep in shade,
  Through far back years of good and ill.

The old grey home of a stalwart race,
  Had answer'd quick all fierce alarms
Of Border foe and midnight raid,
  By call of cresset flame to arms.

In the dim past the first Le Vache
   Brought name and crest from Gascony,
Where sweeps by vine-clad slopes Garonne,
   Bright circling, to the sunny sea.


And one, a valiant Garter Knight,
   Held Calais 'gainst all France's power;
His worn and fading banner hangs
   In the Great Hall of Windsor Tower.


In David's time, and Bruce's wars,
   Were high emprises nobly done;
And knightly honours grandly gain'd
   By knightly deeds of sire and son.


A Vache the Douglas' mythic sword,
   "For Tineman forg'd by fairy lore,"
O'er Scottish hill and English plain,
   And through far lands, stout-hearted bore;

B

Ev'n he who won fair Sinton's tower
   To his lov'd lord the Douglas leal,
Stood by his side at Homildon,
   And shar'd one death at Verneuil.

Dark mem'ries, too, of Border feuds,
   When hand to hand the fight was crav'd,
A face upturn'd to the breaking dawn,
   Dead by the Tweed, but honour sav'd.

A mother sought him on the haugh,
   She found him near the white flower'd thorn ;
The grass red wet ; the heedless birds
   Pip'd sweet strains to the early morn.

And in still nights on upland moor,
   Where runlets of the burn heads croon,
Steel stroke on helm hew'd glints of light,
   Beneath the gleam of the peaceful moon,

That look'd with love on the stricken dead.
    Shedding a calm on the clay cold face,
The agonies and strife of earth,
    Sublim'd by touch of Heaven's grace.


Long chequer'd years of history
    Had made a proud vaunt of the name.
On many a field the pennon shone—
    " By deeds do we extend our fame."


" Five hundred years have come and gone,
    The Scots' Crown has been lost and won.
They are waiting on the hill will tell
    The Dawyck race is now undone."


So said the weird; the old Laird felt
    A heavy soreness at the heart ;
He had known an ingrate King and Court,
    And eke the thankless patriot's part.

The gloamin', creeping on from Scrape,
    Was mingling now its eerie shade
With the grass green knowe where Dawyck Lairds
    Those many hundred years were laid.

In hollow of the soughing burn,
    'Tween old grave mound and high grey Peel,
The Laird saw there the awsome sight,
    Which death alone made him reveal.

"The Weird of Dawyck came on me there,
    The awsome weird that boded ill;
I saw, what no one ever saw,
    The dread white faces of the hill.

" Heads, bodiless heads, one after one,
    Grew from the grey and shapeless air.—
Death's shadows, by one living man
    In ghastly line were fronted there.

" "Tween earth and heaven they hover'd dread.
   The wavering shapes from the unseen ;
As if death pal'd the face of life,
   Or life lent breath to what had been.


" The bodiless heads, they spake no word,
   Pass'd beck'ning in the gloamin' still ;
Oh ! how each turn'd and look'd on me,
   The dread white faces of the hill.


" Of earthly forms no one was there,
   But they I knew were my own race ;
For the saddest look in all the band,
   Was on my own dead father's face.


"Five hundred years have come and gone.
   The Scots' Crown has been lost and won,
They are waiting on the hill will tell
   The Dawyck race is now undone.

"And sore I fear our vaunt is vain,

 'By deeds do we extend our fame,'

And Vache of Dawyck will be, erelong,

 On his forefather's hills but a name."

# MANORHEAD

An urn-round hollow'd glen, clos'd deep within
Its hills, that rise in smoothest symmetry.
To make for it a quiet arch of sky ;
A glen, in far past times deep-fill'd, and scoop'd
By ever-grinding ice, and wind-borne rain,—
The beauteous sculpture of the Unseen Hand
That guides insentient and unthinking powers
To Art's great purpose, through the ages dim,
And 'mid the darkness of the winter nights.

Its arch of sky in summer noon beholds,
From blue, calm height, the quiet depth below,

With heaven's unbroken glory grandly fill'd.

And then, from sparse white fleeting clouds there fall

Tremulous shadows on the pastoral green,—

As passing sadness on a beauteous face,—

That speed a-down the hill-sides, o'er the hollows,

And mingle with the fitful rush of burns,

And the pathetic voice of bleating lambs.


Again, the hollow urn with deep mist fills,

And veils its splendour, yet gives forth a sound

Of hidden waters from its depths remote,

As if the Spirit of the hills had there

Withdrawn within himself, to hold lone musing,

Deep murmuring o'er the secrets of the glens.


But now, a breath from heaven cleaves through the
     mist,

And bares before the ardent eye blue rifts

Of sky, and sunny slopes of mottled hills;

And then, the west'ring sun strikes slantingly,

And with a golden tide the glen o'erflows,

Of shimm'ring splendour, short-liv'd, fast pursued

Across the hollow, up the radiant slope

By hast'ning evening shadow, until at length

Day's one last passionate glow burns on the brow

Of the sun-fronting height, and passes thence

For ever into gloamin' of the moor.

# MANOR WATER

In its far glen, Manor outspreads its arms
To all the hills, and gathers to itself
The burnies breaking from high mossy springs,
And white streaks that fall through cleavings of the crag
From lonely lochans, where the curlews cry
And sweep o'er peaty water round blench'd stones
That speak the ceaseless alchemy of years ;
And well-eyes fring'd with fair Forget-me-not,
That here, in purest hue and slender'st form,
Wears the soft passion of its pleading face,—
Sweet child of Nature, straying in the wild,
Fearless in power of gentle grace to win
The mountain spirit, and charm him from his rudeness

In gather'd strength, leaps Manor to free life.

Then loves, in sweetest winding waywardness,

To stray and gleam amid the grassy haughs,

From foot of green to foot of heather hill;

Now hiding coy beneath the fringed bank,

Then rushing forth and breaking into joy

Amid the sun-bright music of its stones;

Then hast'ning under drooping alder leaves,

Whose shadows float with ripples of the stream:

On, ever on, 'mid links of fair green haughs,

Circling around sedate old wooded farm-steads,

Each list'ning in hush'd stillness to its burn

That rises high upon its quiet hill,

And croons half-hid adown its bracken glen.


Enfolding Castlehill's old crumbling peel,

With lichens brown, and hollow-eyed, owl-haunted,

A hoary memory from the far dim past;

Sweet Well-bush, clasp'd in hollow of the hill,

Forsaken home, now but a winsome name
Amid its wood and by its fresh green spring,
Where fleeting shapes are seen at early morn,
But hide them in the hush of open noon,
Yet hint a secret presence in the shade.

Lo! ancient Woodhouse, with the Bow'd Dwarf's cot,
Where from his bole the awsome form peer'd grim
On passer-bye,—weird as the old world life
He lived, and lore he knew,—strangely akin
In shape and mien to those dread eerie things,
That find soul solace on the stony moor,
And haunt moon-shadow'd hollows of the hills;
And Manor Kirk and Kirkyard where he lies,
Even in his grave safe kept from witches' spell,
His life-long dread, by charm of rowan tree.

Cademuir, dear hill, around thy grassy slopes,
Long dallies Manor in its lingering folds,

And breathes upon thee gentle ev'ning mists,

That thou may'st charm us with the earliest green,

And clothe thyself in many blended hues,

Glad now in sunny sparkle of the stream,

In gloamin' wan as is the water's face.


Free Nature here has work'd her fullest will,

And wove her contrasts with a skilful hand,

Mix'd soft and stern, the gentle and the wild,

Set grace in loving mood at grandeur's feet;

Fus'd strength of hills, and charm of verdant haugh,

And gleam of stream, and shadows of the glens;

Set in rare symmetry broad mountain brows,

Whose dark and ruddy glow of heather bloom,

Is streak'd and lit by blinks of tender green,-

Soft growing pasture and the bracken sheen,—

And crown'd by waving locks of lint-fair bent,

That from the Summer snatching sunny hues,

Wear them through Autumn and the fading year.

Hills guard the strath and shut out all but heaven,

And flow and fall in wavy lines, and meet

In one amid the wild flowers of the vale,

Where bending woodruff sheds a sweet perfume.

And fragrant thyme floats on the charmed air;

And o'er the whole there sleeps a summer calm,

Made deeper by the gentle noise of streams,—

As breath of holy thought and gracious feeling,—

For here the peace of heaven hath fallen, and here

The Earth and Sky are mute in sympathy.

From Cademuir to the water head,
  Where far heights meet the arching sky,—
Light azure, crossed by lines of red,—
  On each side, broad white hill tops lie;

Hills facing hills, rob'd pure in snow,
  White gleaming in the frosty sun,—
In long fair slopes descending low
  To glens of umber'd shadow dun.

Hush'd in the vale is every tone,—
  No cry of beast, no note of bird,—
Save where the bursting stream alone,
  Makes its full voice be hoarsely heard;

And as it breaks in circling round,
　It sweeps the snowy hills the while,
With deeper than its summer sound,—
　With flashes of its summer smile.


It seems to let the winter rest,
　Rest quietly on hill and lee,
With hope full swelling in its breast,
　Again the summer sun to see,—


Once more to be itself again,
　Once more to lave the summer green,
Once more to light the purple glen,
　And glance beneath the willow sheen.


This is in truth thy lot, fair stream,
　When each bare winter time is o'er,
To bask in April's gracious gleam,
　And joy in summer's bounteous store.

Cycles of change in ceaseless flow,
　　Unresting as thy coursing tide,—
Knowest thou that they come and go,
　　And dost thou ask why none abide?


Thou art but each; we more than all;
　　However constant seasons flow;
As light and shade upon earth's wall,
　　We see them come,—we see them go.


The Spirit in us weaves in one,
　　The many cycles of the years;
The sad regrets of times now gone,
　　Our present longings, future fears.


We grasp the change,—we feel it flow
　　Through winter tides and summer dells;
And thus in inmost heart we know
　　The absolute soul within us dwells,—

Within us dwells and feels the power
Of Nature in its every mood ;
One whether it in winter lower,
Or sweetly prank the summer wood.

The long full sense in human life
Of Thought which us the god-like brings,
Recks nothing of the changing strife
Of Nature and unconscious things.

For Thought will rise a future spring,
Fair as the Spring on Manor glen,
With tend'rest hue of living thing,
That ne'er will fade in hearts of men.

## MARGARET TWEEDIE
## OF DRUMMELZIER

Of fierce, rapacious race she came,
  Fair Margaret Tweedie, maiden mild
And meek, as her forefathers aye
  Were violent, lawless, stern, and wild.

As graceful harebell sweetly rears
  At foot of old gnarl'd elm its form,
'Neath rugged bole and knotted bough,
  Grown grim through centuries of storm :

So she, last of Drummelzier's line,
  Burst from the stock in beauty free.
The marvel that so fair a flower
  Should spring up 'neath so rude a tree.

A shade oft passed o'er that fair face,
  Though eighteen summers scarce had roll'd,
To mould her graceful form, and lend
  Their glimmer to her locks of gold.


"And must I leave the sparkling Tweed,
  The cradle of Drummelzier's line,
My father's peel tower 'mid the wood,
  The meadow sweet, the lowing kine,


"The sunny birk far up the burn,
  That twines close with the rowan tree,
Beneath whose shade I sat and play'd,
  When far I stray'd in childhood free.


"Upon a simple timid lass,
  As feeble as the hill-side fern,
Has come a weighted load of ill,
  Too great for oak old, strong, and stern.

" A ruin'd house, a broken name,—
        Thus years of strife, and years of blood,
    Have grown into the frown of Heaven,
        And burst on me as thunder-cloud.


"Oh! could I wield my father's sword,
        Or lift up my dead brother's spear,
    I know from pulsing of my blood,
        My mother's age were guarded here.


" Why did I dream that winsome dream,
        When face and form were figur'd there,
    The gracious face, the stalwart form,
        With steel casque o'er his yellow hair?


" I lay beneath the burnie's birks,
        That were abowing o'er my eyne,
    I saw his shadow on the pool,
        I saw him dusk the sunny sheen.

".A passing form o' the misty hill,

    A gleaming glint o' the sun-lit glen,

    He cross'd this weary life of mine,

        I fear 'twill ne'er be bright again!


"Oh God! would I had touch'd that hand,

    Oh God! would I had kiss'd that face,

    Ere it had gone for once and aye

        Into the drear void blank of space."


A message came to Margaret's bower,—

    Two mail-clad men are in the hall,—

    "The end is near; God give me grace,

        And strength, and heart to bear our fall."


The father, he was grim in mien,

    Outspoke his purpose hard and cold;

    "No Tweedie now sits in this tower,

        Drummelzier owns me for its lord."

Ah! little reck'd she what he said,

  For Sight and Memory thrilling were,

By look of that young gracious face,

  With steel casque o'er his yellow hair.


The vision 'neath the burnie's birks,—

  The web of Fate was now unwound;

Both face and form she knew them well,—

  And these two souls in one were bound.


She needed not her father's sword;

  She needed not her brother's spear:

A fair face won the young laird's heart,

  And age and youth are guarded here.

## A WINTER SCENE

This morn the dim and wading sun,
  The grey-cold sky, the shadowy wood,
That wavers 'mid the creeping haze,
  Low trailing like a broken cloud,

Bode soon the snow-drift; slow it comes;
  Then fast in flow, flapp'd by the wing
Of North-east blast that wheels and whirls,
  O'er earth's face, strong in eddying ring.

Now lowers it, dark'ning all the sight,
  Then rises with low deep'ning sound,
Flake flutters after fluttering flake,
  In ever-changing ceaseless round.

So wayward moves the atom dance,
   So swift and fierce its circling course,
'Twould seem as if the winter air
   Were shiver'd by rude spirit force.

Snow thickens by the river's brink,
   Snow floats upon its bosom wide,
The white marge meets the water wan,
   That sweeps in wild and wintry tide.

How little like that gentle stream
   That flow'd in summer's twilight hour,
O'er shadows, motionless as death,
   Of rock and tree and lone grey tower.

Amid its deep encircling woods,
   Old Neidpath rears its roof of snow,
As it has done through countless years,
   When storms were loud, and suns were low.

Hills dim and distant gird us round,
 Their wavy lines half-seen, half-hid,
They rise into the winter storm,
 They melt in vast infinitude.


Ah, hills! I love you at all times,
 I love you in your summer days,
When glints of light are on your face,
 And heather blooms athwart your braes.


But now you touch the soul far more,
 Thus rising dim in misty shroud,
Wild snow-drifts beating round your heads,
 High hill-tops passing into cloud,—


With weird groups in the upper air,
 Old fancies shaped in living form,
That flash forth from the storied past,—
 Flash forth and revel in the storm.

## A MIDNIGHT RAID

A day of quiet cloud and soft sunlight,
And now the sun was down, and forth I went
To watch from neighb'ring hill the beacon-fires
That told a Queen was once again within
The Cheviot line that bars the Border land.
A mile or two of road, and then the hill
Is reach'd, and, as upon the height I rise,
Sight-filling, westward, Tinto's great broad mass.
Looms dark against the purple evening sky;
And, fronting him, Cardon and Culter Fell.
His worthy peers, in silence rounded lie:
From west to east, encompassing the sight,
Dim shapes of hills, broad-bosom'd, faintly set:
The wavy line of Pentlands northward runs
Athwart a belt of cloud, beneath a sky

Of pale and fading light; the heights in front

Fade slow before me in the evening mist;

Behind, down in the vale there lies one gleam,

A break of Tweed, lov'd stream of early days,

Now shining out sole light of all the earth;

Around, the full flush'd heather fades to grey;

Amid the dark, the grouse-cock springs and crows ;

White, staring, startled sheep together rush,

And flee in groups; below, a slender mist,

And sound of rushing water companies

Me all unseen; o'erhead, pale light of stars.

At length the height is gain'd, and lo ! aflame

Is all the Border Land; the hills, fire-topp'd,

Rise high against the misty weather-gleam,

And ruddy all the circling crown of heaven;

Blaze Caldcleugh Head and bale of Ruberslaw,

And well does Teviot know the olden glare,

Shine distant lights on lonely Lammermuirs,

The wizard Eildons flash on fair Melrose,

And Dryburgh, that keeps the sacred dead,

In sympathy has caught the beacon glare

That breaks the shadows o'er the Minstrel's tomb.

The spirit stern of old world life was there,

On wavering face of fell, and ruin'd peel,

And moorland dim, and gleam of mountain burn,

And benty bridle track where reivers rode,

All weirdly blended in that umber'd light.

At length the moon arose, the autumn moon,

In mild effulgence ; bright grew ruddy fires,

And caught clear outline from the mellow beam,

Beneath the pale blue of the higher sky.

In one's heart quiet feelings, thoughts of peace

From symbols of old wars ; the past's dread things

Become our present playthings ; joy for awe ;

What rous'd the blood to stern and fierce resolve,

Now us'd to move it but in calmest course ;

The spirit old of Border Hills unquench'd,

Fire-eyed as aye, and ready for the fray,

In ancient language speaking as of yore,

But with new meaning, flashing festal joy

In need-fire blaze, the flush of welcome bright

O'ermantling all its stern old warrior face.

Once homewards turn'd, the winding plain was gain'd,

Where lay the road 'twixt hedge-rows, bord'ring trees

With heavy leafage, dark against the moon;

On either side were corn-fields, yellowing:

Between the trees the moon gleams streak'd with
    white

The highway, dimly lit the shaded gaps

In hedge-rows, fill'd by busy fancy's forms.

But lo! another sight, a window-lamp,

Descried across the fields, amid the trees,

Kept brightly shining by love's hands, to light

The homeward way, and there a sweet, fair face

Solicitous, and keeping watch at night;

And thus was old romance merg'd readily

In deep pure quietude of home and hearth.

Wild your cradle glen,
   Young Hay of Talla,
Stern the wind's wild roar
Round the old peel tower,
   Young Hay of Talla.


Winter night raving,
   Young Hay of Talla,
Snowy drift smooring,
Loud the Linn roaring,
   Young Hay of Talla.

Aye he heard it rush,
   Young Hay of Talla,
As it swell'd and burst,
Fierce his soul was nurs'd,
   Young Hay of Talla.


Winterhope's wild hags,
   Young Hay of Talla,
Gameshope dark foaming,
There ever roaming,
   Young Hay of Talla.


Hating soft even-tide,
   Young Hay of Talla,
In the deep moon-calm
Finding no soul-balm,
   Young Hay of Talla.

Watch'd keen the wold-fire,
　　Young Hay of Talla,
Soul leapt at wild light
Flash'd on gloom of night.
　　Young Hay of Talla.


A sweet heart betray'd,
　　Young Hay of Talla,
Love's trust cast aside,
Made of her no bride,
　　Young Hay of Talla.


Mary has come and gone,
　　Young Hay of Talla,
Back to marriage ball,
Is God over all,
　　Young Hay of Talla?
D

And you are here, you,
  Young Hay of Talla,
God's heaven above you,
Future before you,
  Young Hay of Talla.


Have you made your choice,
  Young Hay of Talla?
Turn'd quite from Heaven's gate,
Taken the fiend's fate,
  Young Hay of Talla?


Night round Kirk o' Field,
  Young Hay of Talla,
Light faint in the room,
Darnley sleeps in gloom,
  Young Hay of Talla.

Heavy the oaken stair,

  Young Hay of Talla,

Light there your foot-fall,

See none answers call,

  Young Hay of Talla.


Shadow by bed-side.

  Young Hay of Talla,

Noise in the dull dark,

Does sleeper now hark.

  Young Hay of Talla?


Yes! sure he moves! Yes!

  Young Hay of Talla.

Grasp the living throat.

Have you the grip got,

  Young Hay of Talla?

Ah! the young form moves,
   Young Hay of Talla,
Hold him grim,—hold grim,
Till quivers not a limb,
   Young Hay of Talla.


Now the dread deed's done,
   Young Hay of Talla,
Throw the corpse o'er the wall,
Give it dead dog's fall,
   Young Hay of Talla.


High before heaven,
   Young Hay of Talla,
Standing this winter morn,
Ah, how sore forlorn!
   Young Hay of Talla.

Reaping a life's fruit,
  Young Hay of Talla,
Getting no man's ruth,
Passing, oh ! where, in youth,
  Young Hay of Talla ?

Begg'd the dishonour'd dead,
  Young Hay of Talla,
She you made no bride,
Laid you by Talla-side,
  Young Hay of Talla.

## AULD DAUNDER LATE

A queer auld wife was Daunder Late,
In wee hoose by itsel', on the moor,
Naebody e'er cam' near the door,
    The lane door o' auld Daunder Late.

A wizzen'd wife was Daunder Late,
Wi' grey cloak, stick, and twa grey een,
Peering frae under her brows, sae keen,
    Grisly brows o' auld Daunder Late.

Aye oot o' nichts was auld Daunder Late,
Moonshine, or mirk, cauld, weet, or snaw,
Windy or lown, 'twas naething ava',
    Naething ava' to auld Daunder Late.

Out o' the darkest side o' the road,

A' on a sudden she'd start, like fate;

When a' other folks had left the gait,

    Ye would aye find auld Daunder Late.


Naebody could gang o'er the moor,

At night gey eerie e'en at the best,

But ahint some howe, just like a ghaist,

    Whae'd turn up but auld Daunder Late?


When fisher folk gaed oot i' the dark,

Wi' a tarry-licht to burn the stream,

What think ye wad pop out o' the gleam

    Ahint them but auld Daunder Late?


Naebody kenn'd where frae she came,—

A grey wisp o' the norland blast,

That frae the angry cluds was cast,

    Grew, some said, into auld Daunder Late.

But others said she was no frae abune,

She came oot o' the hag o' the moor,

O' the hole they were perfectly sure,

    Sure aboot auld Daunder Late.


Whene'er appear'd the auld wife's cloak,

Ilka bit bairn cleek'd in its thoomb,

And, keeking round, gae her plenty room,

    Fearing the witch auld Daunder Late.


"A witch, ye gowks," growl'd Daunder Late,

"Can I be a witch, and no ken o't?"

That was a' ony ane ever got,

    Ever got frae auld Daunder Late.


But fine instinct led baith young and auld

To think, as genius canna tell,

The great power it may have in itsel',

    It might be sae wi' Daunder Late.

What puzzl'd Jock Brown and a' the folk,
Whae would make the ways o' Heaven clear,
Was hoo' she was permitted here
    Sae lang to tarry, auld Daunder Late.


Ae thing I ken o' auld Daunder Late,
She was aye to me a fearsome wife,
Whether or no she belanged to this life,
    A fearsome wife auld Daunder Late.

## WILL SAW THE FAIRIES

Up in far Glensax,
Where the burn leaves hags,
Scoops out the deep crags,
   Will saw the Fairies.

Grand glints in the glen,
Heather and brackens deep,
Rounding the burn's sweep,
   Lov'd by the Fairies.

He an angler lone,
Listing the pool's tune,
On bright day at noon,
   Will saw the Fairies.

Watching his line fall,
Heard behind him clear,
Notes as of pipes near,
    Pipes of the Fairies.


Turn'd him round about,
Saw one in mantle green,
Sitting 'mid grassy sheen,
    Round him the Fairies.


Old and quaint he was,
Pip'd he soft and sweet,
Dancing with swift feet,
    Round him the Fairies.


East and west Will look'd,
Down threw rod and creel,
Head began to reel,
    Will saw the Fairies.

Away down the burn,
Rush'd he in wild state,
Telling his strange fate,
  Will saw the Fairies.


But faith was lacking,
Green the knowe and bare,
Nothing they saw there,
  Couldn't see the Fairies.


No more to lone Glensax,
Will brought creel and rod,
Nor there was turt trod,
  Trod e'er by Fairies.


Ah ! what we might know,
Could we bear the gleam
That lights dark life's stream,
  Will saw the Fairies.

## *ALTA MONTIUM:*

### *AMONG THE UPLANDS*

Far back in early youth, a fount of song,

Of simple, artless song, burst from his heart,

As first upwelling pure of mountain rill;

A mother's lore had taught him old-world strains,

Unknown in books, yet natural as the airs

That play among the tender flowers of glens,

And often thrilling, as the wandering sounds

That strangely rise and die on upland moor;

And he had visions brief of things that were,

In broken legend and dark half-told tale,

That awed the heart, gave wing to eager thought;

As weird and wondrous depths of hills disclos'd,

For but a moment, through a rift of mist,

And then involv'd, to eye of wanderer
On lonely height, in blank bewildering gloom,
When all is left to fear and phantasy:
And touching stories, too, of life and death,
The joys and sorrows of our human lot,
In old grey houses that are roofless now,
Silent to children's voice and evening psalm,
Or sunk beneath green mounds, one sycamore
Still stretching out its wide and leafy boughs
Before the sun, in vain and vacant shade.

An undertone of feeling this became,
Scarce conscious, and yet fus'd with course of thought.
Aye sounding dimly in the haunted ear,
As croon of burn that, half-hid, sings its song
In hidden circlings 'neath a grassy fringe,
And is the life at heart of the green glen.
For, meanwhile, he had gone into the land
Of abstract thought, to strive with problems dark

Of Man and God, of Nature and Free-Will,

Of destiny, beginning absolute,

And issue infinite of things, of forms

Of Intellect, Desire, and Feeling :--world

Of thought transcendent, whose powerful spell

Both dread and daring, holds the vision pure,

And high imagining at eager stretch,

Through mystery, through reverence and awe,

And haunting feeling of the limitless.


Like bow o'erbent returning to the straight,

Elastic to his native wilds he sprung,

And there would be long days among the hills,

Rejoicing in far, breezy, upland heights,

The beauty free of purple moorland bloom ;

Haunting those lone recesses where the burns

From high green grassy springs creep slowly forth,

Above the cleavings of the deep red scaurs,

To scoop the hollow glen, and joyous leap

Through sunny fall to strong, deep, eddying pool;
There thrown aside all reason-grounded doubts,
All narrow aims, and self-regarding thoughts,
Out of himself amid the infinitude,
Where Earth, and Sky, and God are all in all.

And joy he found in fairy spots of burns,
Where solitary birch, rock-rooted, droops,
And drapes with lightsome shadows from its leaves,
A lone linn-pool, that sings a song unheard,
Far up among the hills; or where a rowan,
Set high against a bit of azure sky,
Hangs out its berries red in deep ripe flush
Of waning Autumn, 'mid its yellowing leaves,
Each quivering with light motion of its own,
While all the air is still in calm of noon.

In other graver mood would tarry long
Where massive forehead of the hill is scor'd,

And holed by deep dark hollow'd peaty hags,

Eyeless, and sullen to the sun and heavens;

And broken mounds, scant-sprinkled with hill grass.

As wasting islands on the mountain slope,

Lie 'mid the sluggish oozing of black rills,

The slow but sure down-wearers of the world;

All speaking revel fierce in winter nights,

When wild winds rave and tear across the moor,

And sounding torrents hurry down the hills,

And misty shapes of storm stalk high in air,

Their foot-prints leaving in the cloven hags,

Now hush'd and laid by charm of summer time.


Came soothing musings of an afternoon,

As slowly in the west the sun went down,

And great sky splendour lay beyond the hills

That long in outline barr'd the western heaven;

For then vast shadows of great crags, and high

Broad hollow'd scaurs, fell long across the glens,

E

And o'er the lower hill tops, and lay calm
On faintly darken'd greenery of haughs;
The valleys filling with a tremulous air
Of blue clear mist, that veil'd the mountain wall,
Until through growing fusion earthly mass
Commingled, and was lost, in pure ethereal form.

And often, 'mid that golden evening calm,
When daundering down the hill-side from the west,
'Mid fore-stretch'd shadows, and the softening forms
Of hills, and gleams of waters in the glens,
And quiet circling smoke, that rising spake
Of rest to man and beast, and hush of toil
On farm-stead,—wrapt in soothing mild sun-glow;—
Such scenes as these took deep hold of the heart,
And shaped themselves in quiet phantasy,
As gleaming spots 'mid other graver thoughts,
To mental eye well-pleasing, as to sense
Appears a gracious field of yellow grain,

On hill-face hanging high, like golden shield,
'Mid deep, broad, bordering of dark fir-woods.
These fill'd the sphere of vision of the soul,
And sooth'd the yearning instincts of the heart,
For sensuous symbols of unclothëd thoughts,
For colour, form, and emphasis of sense,
Wherein there came to full and conscious life,
Emotions, aspirations, and desires,
Before felt but as powers of dim unrest,
In depths infinite of the heart we are.

'Twas thus he came to learn how near akin
The forms and scenes of simple Nature are
To truest Art; how nature-feeling free
Is quickening soul of art, that teaches us,
And lives for men; how Poesy may grow
Within the heart, and joy in imaging
What mere wild nature keeps but for herself,—
The glow of heathery brae, and bracken leaf,

Fair grasses slender, bending to soft airs,
The many-colour'd mosses by spring wells,
The pale hill violets that wear kind looks,
Tracery delicate in green secret spots,—
With which impassion'd and pure heavenly love
Hath bless'd the poor lot of the barren moor,—
The gleaming burn that wimples 'mid green folds,
The soft and wayward winds that stray a-musing,
And fitful waters echoing from grey rocks,
Among the earless and untrodden hills.

He felt how fading Beauty still can charm
By Pathos, when first streaks of autumn-fall
Tell that another cycle of green life
Is passing from the sun and fair-fac'd earth;
Birks up the glens, enwrapt in golden fold,
And brackens round their roots pale yellowing,
The evening glory of their passing day;
And lightsome fairy spots of sunny bent,

That make a gracious splendour on the moor,

All through the wane of the declining year,

Until the wild winds come, and sough, and fall,

And all hill-glory of the year grows dim;

And then the golden grass foregoes its hue,

And blench'd as hair, when hoary eld has come,

It flutters sparse amid the breaking mist,

And bows its head to the resistless death,

That falls on things from ever flowing years.


He felt how out of Terror Grandeur grows;

How sense of self, and danger, and dread pain,

First wakes in presence of the mighty hill,

Unfathom'd glen, deep flood, and moorland wide;

How mother Nature's sterner face we fear,

And Fancy conjures, in the driving mist,

Dark giant forms that weirdly haunt the hills,

Take shape, dislimb, amid the hurrying wreaths;

Hears elritch sounds far down in depths of glens,

And dreaded voices in the wailing winds ;

Sees stern fix'd faces glaring through the rifts

Of storm that trail across the hill-side scaurs,

As if dread living shapes were lurking there,

Keen peering through grey eyes of riven hills ;

And, in the downward rush of mountain burn,

Hears dreaded water-spirit joy or wail,

In varying struggle with the mortal man

Who dares the venture of the angry flood.


All this he felt, and how the thought of self,

And self-regarding fear, lose all their power,

Through constant haunting of the great broad hills,

Through the dread joy at heart of solitude,

The infinite sense of earth-o'er-arching sky ;

How free wild Nature grows into a love,

And holds the heart by the stern tie of awe,

And sense of the sublime, where welling joy

Comes in the place of fear, yet keepeth still

The element of pain, as a faint shade
That may subdue the too-exulting heart,
And teach how near akin are joy and grief,
And all the primal movements of our souls.


How natural fear may lose its chilling power,
And terror grow to pure æsthetic sense,
The heart may learn in depths of lone Glenrath,
As looking to its burn-heads there are seen
Long sky-lines flowing over massy breadths
Of hills that wall you round in crescent fold,
And run in rapid flow down from high heaven,
To sombre glens, whose slopes are consecrate
For aye to grandeur, solitude, and awe;
Whence seem to slide steep grey-blue breaks of stones,
Yet rest midway, scant studded by dark spots
Of clasping heather; under mighty bulk
And power of shadow, and the stillness deep,
And stern grey look, you seek relief to sense

In the bit blue of sky beyond the height,—
All that is left of heaven by mass of earth,—
Or find companionship, 'mid loneliness,
In sparse white sheep that, sprinkled far below,
In pastoral quiet crop the green burn-braes.

And deep was Fancy mov'd when first was seen
The old brown-bridle track that takes its rise
At low burn-ford, and by long circling ways
Leads up the hill 'mid heather, crowfoot green,
As elfland path, winding round fernie brae,
Away across the broad and breezy height,
O'er hill, down glen, and through the peat-moss deep,
Cross unbridg'd burn and water, skirting lochs,
Past old peel towers that crumble by its side,—
Dun faded line, as story of the past.
For back then rush'd his thoughts to olden time,
When it was trod o' nights in soft moonlight,
Or under pale starr'd sky, by reivers rude,

On whose hearts hardly fell the peace of heaven :

For nothing loath they were, if hot pursued,

To curse the bright blinks of the sacred moon;

But scann'd with keen, unfaltering eye the shape

That ominous chanc'd to loom before them dark

Against the weather-gleam 'twixt hill and sky,

And catching eager every wakening sound

That seem'd to stir behind them in the glen,

Where fierce pursuers, with the sleuth-hound red,

Relentless follow'd, only stayed with blood.


There king and kingly retinue have pass'd,

In gayest bravery, on to forest chase;

Long lines of lords and ready vassals pour'd,

Face southward turn'd, all boune for Border war.

There monarch stern, with purpose keen and hard,

Rode regally to Cockburn's lonely tower,

And left the widow wailing o'er her knight,—

That passionate wail, as if the heart of life

Then beat its strongest throb, and after puls'd
In low consenting fall to welcome death.


And by it on sweet Sabbath morns long gone,
Folks wended to St. Mary's Forest Kirk,
Where mass was said, and matins, softly sung,
Were borne in fitful swell across the Loch ;
And full of simple vision, there they saw,
In Kirk and Quire, the brier and red rose
That fondly met and twin'd o'er lovers' graves,
Who fled o' night through moor up Black Cleugh
        heights,
Pass'd through the horror of the mortal fight,
Where Margaret kiss'd a father's ruddy wounds,
Fled from dead faces pallid on the knowe,
So sadly shadow'd by the soft moonlight.


And some in that quaint time perchance had been
Around the oaken bier, with silver lin'd,

That had been carried far from southern land,

On which the pallid maiden lay all night,

White robed for burial; but, on the morn,

When dead bell stirr'd sad echoes o'er the loch,

And sweet fac'd maidens came to mourn her youth,

At magic touch of lover's hand, grew bright

As lily flower, and, with fair rosy cheek

And ruby lip, sweet smil'd upon her knight.


Strange stories linger'd in those lonely glens,—

Of that weird eve when wizard Binram old,

Was laid in drear unrest, beyond hallow'd ground;

How, at bell-tolling by no mortal hand,

And voices saying words which no man knew,

There rose such shrieks from low depths of the
    lake,

And such wild echoes from the darken'd hill,

That holy men fled from the scant fill'd grave,

And left bare buried that unholy priest.

And they who went by that dim bridle track,

And worshipp'd ardent in the old lone kirk,

Had other faith than that they learnt from priest,

Faith that grew up among their native wilds;

For fervid Phantasy, art unfulfill'd

Of Poesy, was in their simple hearts,

And peopled for them links of green on hills,

And sunny glimmer of the birken shaw,

And yellow broom on braes of burnies clear,

And soft green knowes that cover'd secret halls,

With fairy folk, that rode in mantles green,

That pass'd and revell'd light and free as wind;

Laugh'd elritch laughter up 'mong lonely crags;

That had no care, and knew no solemn thought,

And rose above our chequer'd human lot,

As they o'erleapt the limits of our power,

To life of pleasure all unmix'd with pain;

And all regardless of what awes the heart,

For often, when the north wind tore the bent

At dead of night, lone traveller on moor
Would hear their bridles ring, and hear them flout,
With frolic sound of oaten pipe, bog-reed,
And hemlock clear, the eeriness around.


But lessons high of faith, self-sacrifice,
Lay in the lorn and mythic Fairies' creed.
For ah ! if mortal knight caught by their spells,
That they might through him pay the awful teind
Of sacrifice, each seventh year, to hell,
How hard to pluck him from their mystic hold !
For at dread midnight hour on Hallow Eve,
The lover maid must wait on lonesome moor,
Her only strength and hope the cross of stone,
That looms dim-grey between her and the sky;
Must list the elritch sounds that there foretell
The weird on-coming of the unearthly troop,
That clang forth from the hollow of the hill,
Until the air becomes possess'd with sound,

Her heart first quailing at the growing clang,

Then swelling strong with hope of lover sav'd;

Watch signal from her knight, and hold him there.

Whate'er he turn, be it the loathsome newt,

Or adder, or a bale within her arms,

Or red-hot gad of iron, still struggling hard

In fight with lover's will possess'd, and turn'd

Against himself, his love, and his own heart;

Till victory falls to faith and stern resolve,

And vanish fearful forms and gruesome shapes,

With which the powers ot ill can blinding clothe

The substance of our highest, purest good.


On summer morn, in that old time, as now,

The mist would fill the hollow of the Loch,

Then wreathe in twain, and softly rise and glide

Up hill-sides green, and then the water still

Unbared its gleam, as touch'd by splendour rare

Of sun and sky; or toward evening fall,

When hill-tops round are radiant, it would lie
Hush'd in soft shade below the Forest Kirk ;
Then listen to aye deep'ning sough of burns,
As in the dusk they puls'd down moon-streak'd hills,
All through the silent air; but, of that time,
No one hath caught or limn'd the Loch's still face
That sought in vain the way to human hearts
Awed into fear by its dread loneliness.
Perchance in calm of Sabbath afternoon,
When holy thoughts were in the heart, and when
Dark passions had been laid by sacred hymn,
Some finer soul might feel the soothing scene,
And quiet eye be charm'd, as now, by spell
Of gleaming water, and deep mirror'd hills.

But feeling full the spirit of the time
Rude, bold, and daring, with shadows of dark deeds
On all the glens, men in soul sympathy
Would pause to view the Loch's tumultuous mood,

When down the Hopes the south-west winds would
    roar,
And drive white lines of foam in crested flow
Along the hurrying sweep of waters dark,
Barring from shore to shore the raging Mere ;
For strange vague power to sense was imag'd there,
Which, when it loses force of threat'ning fear,
Becomes refined to soul of the sublime.

And later, in deep spirit-stirring times,
Folks sought the hollow of the cloven hag,
' Mid Winterhope's grey wreaths of sheltering mist,
Where Renwick told of one great sacrifice,
Ere he himself had borne in full his cross,
And hearts sublimed were round him in the wild,
And faces, God-ward turn'd in fervent prayer,
For deeply smitten, suffering flock of Christ ;
And clear uprose the plaintive moorland psalm,
Heard high above the plover's wailing cry,

From simple hearts in whom the spirit strong
Of hills was consecrate by heavenly grace,
And firmly nerv'd to meet, whene'er it came,
In His own time, the call to martyrdom.

And still there may be seen, on that dim track,
Memorial solemn that our human heart
Is link'd on to the past in life and death,
When shepherd old in plain deal coffin laid,
With plaid for pall spread o'er the rustic cart,
Is slow borne to the lonely hill of graves,
To share the peace of his forefathers' sleep :
Content, in life and death, with simple lot;
Now joyous with the hills in God's sunshine,
Then still'd to solemn thought whene'er they hid
Their faces reverent in His awful storm ;
A daily duty done all through the years,
And now the sum is his sole monument.

F

# MERLIN SYLVESTRIS

O Merlin! woodland Merlin! Sweeter name
Was never feigned for nature-worshipper—
Of fragrant birks and forest greenery
All redolent.  Now, where the birks have been,
Thy name still lingers,—lingers 'mid brown heath,
Green herbage spots, grey stones, and lochans dark,
And voices rare of birds, and tiny eyes
Of gentle flowers that timorously peep
On sterile moor, the orphans of the wild;
True wizard ever thou hast been to me;
Thy name has charm'd the wastes, and sweetly link'd
The present to the past, the seen to the unseen,
The world of sense to that dim shaded sphere
Where fancy stretches forth to spirit forms;

For often in the mist thee have I seen
As, with blown hair, and with weird gleaming eyes,
That flash'd doubt, dark despair, and sore unrest,
Thou had'st fled newly from dread Arderydd.--
Companion of the blank and wandering winds,
Face upward turn'd to breaks of high blue heaven,
If haply they are there,—the Dead, the Dead!


A vision thou of childhood's earliest days,
As phantom-like as wonder-loving youth
E'er joyed in, airy-shap'd as misty forms
On high Drummelzier's broad and breezy Laws,
Wherewith thy fleeting being aye was fused;
Yet real to me as thy dark green grave-mound,
Whereby in youth I've sat and heard dear Tweed
And Powsail join for thee their waters clear
In one consenting wail; for thou had'st power
To carry back one's thoughts to times when forms
Mov'd dim in history's far shadowy dawn, -

Unsteady as the landscape of the sky,

Which is, and then dislimbs, and takes new shape,

As it o'erleaps its limit, and becomes

Another than itself, through shading lines,

Now pure in sunlight and now stain'd with storm.


Some weirdly fable Merlin born of maid

And spirit of the air, a devil's son;

Of serpent subtlety and wizard guile

Compact, whose rule of right was serving one,—

The King,—reckless of final laws of good,

His might of art given up to Uther's son

From birth to death; plastic in mortal shape

As fancy of the fiend, or soul's fell aim

To purpose bent of diabolic will:

But not without a sweet regretful touch,

Within his heart, of that still gentleness

Which he had seen on his earth-mother's face.

And yet, although above all carnal love,

He yielded, in fore-knowledge of his fate,

To woman's wiles, reveal'd his secret art,

Not loath, at length, to tell that wizard lore,

Which, through lone life had in his bosom lain

Untold, close locked before all living men,—

A barrier 'twixt him and sweet earthly love,

And true communing with a human heart,—

His soul the fuel to the pride of power,

And love of fame that lustrous glow'd athwart

The forehead of the time, as star in heaven,

Before the wondering worlds, flames high above

Its peers for a brief hour, then, heart out-burnt,

Sinks a chaotic mass of darken'd death.


Thus one day wandering with his Nimiane

In the wide forest of Broceliande,

They sat them down beneath a hawthorn white

That was both high and fair and full of flowers.

And on her lap he loving laid his head ;

Then round him in his sleep nine times she drew

A cerne, nine times enchantments of his art

She plied; and so when he awoke he found

Himself in fairest, strongest tower e'er rear'd

On earth, and a soft lulling landscape round;

But four walls, there, not made of iron or steel,

Timber or stone, all of enchanted air,

Engird him, once the wisest of the wise,

Now, through pierced weakness of the will, become

Of fools most foolish, caught in his own toils :

For he may pass to none, and none to him,

Save she alone, his Nimiane, who gain'd

His secret art; at will, she comes and goes

Within those walls of airy adamant.


And only once since he was prison'd there

Has Merlin's voice been heard by mortal man,

To pierce this earth's clear air; and but his voice,

Himself invisible,—one sad last plaint

To ear of one lone wandering knight, his own
And Arthur's friend, how he had been deceived ;
One plaint of the coarse world's forgetfulness
Of those that pass away,—one sad farewell,—
And then a mournful and unselfish prayer
To seek for him no more 'mong living men.

But not thus pictur'd 'mid his native wilds
Of ancient Cumbria which he lov'd and mourn'd ;
A martyr there of fading Druid creed,
Yet haunted by a strange remorse and fear,
As if his faith had link'd him to the past,
While in his thought he knew diviner things ;
Among these glens then clothed in birken shaw,
And under hazel shade, glid Merlin seer,
Morvryn's son, and brother of sweet Gwendydd,—
The Dawn,—thus fitly named so pure and fair
Was she ; and he enchanter, wizard, bard,
With art unearthly,—as keen glowing light

That flashes sudden on the moorland waste,—
Gleams up and goes, one knows not whence or
    where,—
And such a chequer'd flame that men recoil
Alike from blessing and from ban in awe.

From human haunts torn by remorse and grief,
Through thought of Arderydd and faces dead,—
King Gwendollew, and well lov'd Gwendydd's
    son,—
That lay upbraiding on that awful field,
Where Pagan Cymry yell'd against the Cross,
By Merlin goaded and his subtle spell;
Until at evening fall scarce one was left
Alive of all that Pagan host, and round
The brighten'd cross, uprais'd, the sun-down glow
From heaven touch'd with pitying smile dead forms
Outstretch'd, of those that from the morn had warr'd
In impotence against the Christlike sign.

Then Merlin, left to dark soul frenzy, fled

Far from the dreaded field of Arderydd,

He knew not where, nor recked, and he was found

Lone haunter of the wood of Caledon ;

Where, hardly shape of earth, rude, naked, wild,

He burst on view of holy Kentigern,

As low he knelt in solitary prayer ;

And when the fearless saint there question'd him,

Said sadly, "Merlin I, the prophet old

Of Gwendollew, who in this solitude

All hardness bear; press ever on my sight

The dead, the dead of Arderydd, my kin,

That lie upturn'd to heaven,—Oh! lie they now

As then, on that dread field 'twixt Liddle's tide

And Carwinelow?—I hear the shrieks that mix'd

With pulses of the stream's unheeding flow.

And woe is me ! I knew the holy Cross,

I knew the Christlike sign was heaven's own gift,

And yet I stood in knowledge against God!"

So Merlin pass'd, and long, long o'er the moor
Re-echoed sad, " The dead of Arderydd."


For forty years and ten, amid the hills
And with the burns, abode the frenzied bard,—
" The fosterer of song among the streams,"—
For aye he clasp'd his harp unto his heart,
Sole solace of his life ; and he would rest
Beside his fountain on the mountain top,
O'ershadowed by the hazels of the hill,
His sad heart soothed by its soft welling sound,
And, gazing eager on the wide woods round,
There, with true poet's soul, he loved to watch
The gambols of the creatures of the wilds,—
The sole companions of his loneliness.


But most he loved and sung the quiet shade
Of that sweet apple-tree of blossoms fair,
Wide-branch'd, and delicate, and beautiful,

That secret grew at Tal Ardd, in the wood,

And by the stream; for its spring leafage waked

Fond memory in his soul, and he would strike

Low soft chords on his harp, strange broken notes.

Like his eye changeful, which now caught, now lost,

The image of an orchard paradise,

His Prince's gift, in old day of courtly fame,

Wherein were seven score and seven blossom'd

    trees,—

A forest grove on a hill's sunny slope;

And therein moved a form, a slender form,—

As glint of sunlight straying 'mong green leaves,—

Fair as first show of blossom on the boughs

In May, ere any wind has rudely blown,

Or frost untimed has frayed its virgin bloom:

And as this phantasm of the past grew dim,

And faded from his sight, in hopeless gloom,

He forceful dash'd, in fury of his heart,

Wild wailing notes upon the echoing air,

And gathering spirits of the hills, dismay'd,
Fled far at hearing of the wildering sound.

'Neath the tree's shade, that by the river grew,
The warrior bard, with shoulder bearing shield,
With sword on thigh, lay calm in vision'd sleep,
And, 'mid the swaying of the river's rush
At night, his soul was soothed; before him clear
Unroll'd was the long course of time to come:
And then he dreamt a sweet dream of a child
Born in the South, who should appear, fair-faced,
Bold as the Sun, when coursing high and strong,
And should upraise the Cymry from their fall;
And with the morn, amid the pleasant notes
Of early birds, beside the gleaming stream
That flowed rejoicing in the tide of dawn,
He took his harp, and in exulting heart
Struck notes prophetic of Cadwallawn's son,
And triumph of the Cymry's ashen spears:

But. as the gloamin' settled on the hill,

The notes were turned again to wailing low,

O'er vision of a youth,—the Cymric hope,—

'Mid wasting pestilence, dead ere his prime.


Yet not alone in those wild wooded hills

Was Merlin old, for haunted was he aye

By mystic female form,—fair Chwifleian,—

Who on him gleam'd in glints of sun through mist,

Then pass'd from view in silent closing wreaths

Of soft hill haur that slowly darken'd o'er

The sky; and she would often secret lurk

In shadows of the birks, and shine in moonbeam

Upon his fountain clear; seeking to enclose

In Polmood's lonely crag the helpless bard,

Where mortal car would ne'er list piteous cry,

But shuddering flee it as an evil wail;

And there to hold him in consentless love,

And come and go whene'er it pleasëd her.

But Meldred's shepherds broke her purpose keen,

And savage slew the weird and wise old man.

And yet they say 'twas but the empty form

That fell beneath the blows of brutal men,

And that in the sad hour of his dire fate,

The haunting spirit, getting now the power

Which she had long'd for, caught the man's true self.

Laid him in bonds of deep enchanted sleep,

In Eildon's halls with Arthur and his knights:

Thence only to awake when ages long

Are gone, and when one, feeling full the heart's

Spontaneous impulse, pure and strong to dare

Oppressive shapes of hideous ill aye quick

To snatch advantage of the faltering will,

Shall fearless draw the sword, then sound the horn,

Amid the darken'd caverns of the hill,

Despite the murmurs of the gathering sprites,

And malisons that fill the muttering air,—

Bold summons back'd by valiant will and deed;—

Then Arthur, Merlin, and the Knights shall rise,

In Eildon's halls, to life and energy,

Feeling once more the spirit of their time,

As morn's reviving breath on misty night,

And with the new-born day in heart rejoice.


Oh! may they come, all cloth'd in dawning fresh

Of the world's fair youth, and bring us back again

To harmony of feeling, word, and deed,

Ideals high, and stirrings of the soul,

That quicken noble work in lives of men,

Unconscious all of self, save as it lives

Sublimed in power abiding and divine

Of simple heart and noble faculty.

# NOTES.

PAGE 1.

### *The Grey Stone on Dollar Law.*

This solitary stone stands as described, on the north-west slope of the Dollar Law (2680 feet). The name is fancifully thought to mean the *Hill of Grief.* The Dollar Law is the eastmost of the crescent ridge of massive mountains—vast, wild, and solitary—that separate the valley of the Tweed from that of the Meggat Water, which flows into St. Mary's Loch. The Grey Stone is one of the oldest monuments in the district. Within these last three years, some one in quest of geological knowledge, with a scientific soul unsoftened by the genius of the place, struck the face of the stone with his excellent hammer, and splintered it to the extent of eighteen inches.

G

### PAGE 1, LINE 4.

#### *Benty.*

*Bent* is a particular kind of hill grass, familiar to all who know the southern uplands. It is constantly referred to in the old ballads as "the Bent sae brown." Brown it may be in late Autumn; in July it is finely sunny, and graceful as wavy golden hair. Hence, perhaps, the name of *Common Hair Grass*.

### PAGE 3, LINE 6.

*Merlin.* See below *Merlin Sylvestris*, page 82, line 1.

### PAGE 4, LINE 14.

#### *Hot Trod.*

The "Hot Trod" was the phrase which indicated the mode of pursuit of a Border marauder who was driving off cattle not his own under shelter of night. It was carried on as here described; and we can quite understand the eagerness and the picturesqueness of the pursuit and flight,—up the glen and over the hills. Hot it must have been for pursued and pursuer.

## PAGE 5, LINE 2.

### *Hope.*

*Hope*, or *Houp*, is a " sloping hollow between two hills, or the hollow that is formed between two ridges on one hill "—*(Jamieson)*. This is the application of the word in the southern uplands of Scotland; but generally, if not universally, it there designates a hollow of the kind described, in which flows a burn, and a *burn* as opposed to a larger stream, or *water*. The valley through which a water flows is usually named a *glen*. At the head of a Hope, too, the hills meet from the opposite sides, and sweep, generally in a curve or crescent form, round the grain or burn head. Otherwise, the opening is called a Glack (Pass). The original idea of Hope is probably enclosure, or enclosed shelter ; as in the hollow between hills. This is confirmed by the use of the word in Lothian and Fife for *haven*,—as St. Margaret's Hope. The runlets, or burns, towards the head of a Hope, are called *Grains*, or *Granes*, because there the main stream divides, or branches out, into several arms or feeders. Grain, according to Jamieson, is literally division, or branch,—from South German *gren-a;* Islandic, *grein-a*, dividere ; *grein*, distinctio.

### PAGE 5, LINE 11.

### *Sough.*

*Sough, souch,*—" a rushing or whistling sound."
Anglo-Saxon, *swæg, swege (Jamieson).* As applied to
a burn or stream, *sough* indicates a fitful rush, or
rise and fall, of water,—a swaying sound familiar to
every one who has listened to the course of a burn
in a glen on a quiet night.

### PAGE 9, LINE 12.

### *Hicht.*

*Hicht,* a height or high hill. *Hichts,* in the plural,
is applied to a range of high and generally massive
hills, as the "Hundleshope Hichts."

### PAGE 10, LINE 1.

### *Stell.*

*Stell,* " an enclosure for cattle, higher than a common fold" *(Jamieson).* The stell, in sheep districts,
is a square or circular dyke (dry stone wall), the area
of which is planted with trees,—generally Scotch firs.
Its use is to afford shelter to sheep in a snow-storm.

Originally it probably meant what is placed or set up,
—from *stellen*, *to place*, or *set*,—hence, *covert*, *enclosure*:
and then it came to denote the particular kind of
enclosure used for sheep or cattle.

### PAGE 12, LINE 1.

### *Trystin'*.

*Tryst*, "an appointment to meet,"—analogous to
*traist*, *trust*.

### PAGE 13, LINE 1.

### *Yirded*.

*Yird*, to cover with earth, or conceal in the earth:
to bury,—from *yird*, earth. "The cauld yird" is
"the cauld grave." Same as *yerd*, *erd*, *erde*, *yerth*.

### PAGE 14, LINE 2.

### *Moorburn*.

Properly *Muir-burn*, or *Mure-burn*,—burning of the
older growth of heath or heather on the moors or
hills, which usually takes place in March.

## PAGE 16.

### *The Weird of Dawyck.*

Dawyck, an ancient estate on the Tweed, was held for nearly five hundred years by a family of the name of Le Vache,—Vache, latterly Veitch. William le Vache signed the Ragman Roll at the Castle of Peebles, in 1296. There were several men of note of this family, to whom reference is made in the text. Sir John Veitch, the second last of the line who held Dawyck, and who is represented as seeing the vision, was Master of Works in Scotland under Charles I., and for a long period a prominent member of the Scotch Parliament. He disinterestedly spent the greater part of his fortune on the repair of public buildings in Scotland, particularly Holyrood, and died an impoverished man, without receiving arrears of salary, recompence, or gratitude. His son had to part with the estate, owing to encumbrances thus contracted, towards the beginning of the eighteenth century.

### PAGE 28, LINE 6.

### *The Bowed Dwarf.*

*Bowed—i.e.,* bent, or crooked, was an epithet of David Ritchie, the original of Scott's "Black Dwarf."

His cottage is in the vale of Manor, and there he spent the greater part of his eccentric life. Unfortunately the exterior of the dwelling has been modernized, and an addition made to it in the form of an adjoining cottage. The garden, however, and the garden wall,—of rough and ponderous stones, put into position almost entirely by his own strength of arm.—remain very much as they were in the time of the dwarf himself. For some details regarding his life and character, see the Introduction to the *Black Dwarf* (1826).

## PAGE 35.

### *Margaret Tweedie of Drummelzier.*

The estate and castle of Drummelzier—for long the possession of the ancient family of Tweedie—passed into the hands of a kinsman, Lord Yester, afterwards first Earl of Tweeddale, about the year 1618. William Hay, Lord Yester's second son, became the new laird; and the tradition is, that when visiting the old tower, with a view to take possession. his heart was touched with pity for the last daughter of the line, whom he made his wife.

## PAGE 43.

### *A Midnight Raid.*

Written August 21, 1867, on the occasion of Her Majesty's visit to the Duke of Roxburghe, at Floors Castle.

## PAGE 47.

### *Young Hay of Talla.*

Talla, probably the Tal Ardd of the *Avallenau* of Merlin, is, especially in its longest reach, where it branches upwards to Gameshope Loch, one of the wildest, most solitary, and most impressive of the south country glens.   Hay, the heir of Talla in Queen Mary's time, was the person who, along with Hepburn of Bolton, strangled Darnley, on Sunday evening, 9th February, 1567, either in the house of Kirk o' Field, or outside of it, as he was endeavouring to escape from his murderers.   Darnley's body was found on the other side of a wall, opposite the chamber in which he had been lying.   The house was blown up by gunpowder, evidently after the king had been put to death.   Young Hay was, no doubt, a relation of the Yester or Tweeddale family, whose principal seat was at that time Neidpath

Castle, on the Tweed. Talla was executed for his part in Darnley's murder, along with his accomplice Bolton, on the 3rd January, 1568. See Burton's *History of Scotland*, IV. 343, V. 93.

## PAGE 73, LINE 2.

*For nothing loath they were, if hot pursued,*
*To curse the bright blinks of the sacred moon.*

> " As Archie passed the Brockwood leys,
>     He cursed the blinkan moon,
> For shouts were borne upo' the breeze
>     Frae a' the hills aboon."

—*Archie Armstrong's Aith* (*Minstrelsy*, III. 481).

## PAGE 73, LINE 6.

*Weather-gleam.*

*Weather-gleam*, or *Weddir glim*, is the clear sky near the horizon, which appears in the twilight or dusk. Anglo-Saxon, *weder*, heaven; and *gleam*, splendour. The weather-gleam appears most markedly in a district where the flowing hill-lines run for a long distance along the horizon. It there looks like a belt or ribbon-line of pale light, between the dark sky above and the dark hills below. An object or person may thus be seen against it at a great distance ; and then looms before the eye in a very impressive manner. The time of night, the indistinctness with which the object is seen, the sharp contrast of light and darkness, are well fitted to give rise to vague suggestions, and feelings of awe in the mind of a solitary traveller on the hills.

PAGE 73, LINE 15.

*There monarch stern, with purpose keen and hard,*
*Rode regally to Cockburn's lonely tower.*

The tradition is, that James V., in 1529, passed by this old Border road, commonly called *The Thieves' Road*, to Henderland tower,—the residence of Piers Cockburn,—and there hanged him as a freebooter, over the gateway of his own tower. That simple, touching, and passionate wail, *The Lament of the Border Widow*, is said to refer to this incident.—See Scott's *Minstrelsy*, II. 322 (ed. 1812).

PAGE 74, LINE 7.

*And, full of simple vision, there they saw,*
*In Kirk and Quire, the brier and red rose.*

The reference is to the *Douglas Tragedy :*

> " Lord William was buried in St. Marie's,
>   Lady Margaret in Marie's Kirk Quire ;
> Out o' the Lady's grave grew a bonnie red rose,
>   And out o' the Knight's a brier."

*Minstrelsy,* II., 224.

### PAGE 74, LINE 16.

*And some in that quaint time perchance had been*
*Around the oaken bier, with silver lin'd.*

See the Ballad of *The Gay Goss Hawk* (*Minstrelsy,* II. 377).

> " She brightened like the lily flower,
>   Till her pale colour was gone ;
> With rosy cheik and ruby lip,
>   She smil'd her love upon."

### PAGE 75, LINE 10.

*Wizard Binram old.*

>                       The wizard's grave ;
> That wizard priest's, whose bones are thrust
> From company of holy dust."

*Marmion ;* Introduction to Canto Second. See also Hogg's Ballad of *Mess John.*

### PAGE 76, LINE 1.

*And they who went by that dim bridle track,*
*And worshipp'd ardent in the old lone kirk,*
*Had other faith than that they learnt from priest.*

The classic Fairy Ballad of the Minstrelsy is *The Young Tamlane*, to which the author is indebted for several phrases, and suggestions of features in the character of the Fairies as here depicted. Janet's heroic and successful attempt to rescue her lover from fairy spell is sung with wonderful simplicity and natural power :—

> " Gloomy, gloomy was the night,
>     And eerie was the way,
>   As fair Janet, in her green mantle,
>     To Miles' Cross she did gae.
>
> " The heavens were black, the night was dark,
>     And dreary was the place ;
>   But Janet stood, with eager wish,
>     Her lover to embrace.
>
> " Betwixt the hours of twelve and one
>     A north wind tore the bent ;
>   And straight she heard strange elritch sounds
>     Upon that wind which went.
>
> " About the dead hour of the night
>     She heard the bridles ring ;
>   And Janet was as glad of that
>     As any earthly thing !

" Their oaten pipes blew wondrous shrill,
   The hemlock small blew clear ;
And louder notes from hemlock large,
   And bog-reed struck the ear ;
But solemn sounds, or sober thoughts,
   The Fairies cannot bear.

    \*      \*      \*      \*      \*

" Fair Janet stood, with mind unmov'd,
   The dreary heath upon ;
And louder, louder wax'd the sound,
   As they came riding on.

" Will o' Wisp before them went ;
   Sent forth a twinkling light ;
And soon she saw the Fairy band,
   All riding in her sight.

" And first gaed by the black, black steed,
   And then gaed by the brown ;
And fast she gript the milk-white steed,
   And pu'd the rider down.

" She pu'd him frae the milk-white steed,
   And loot the bridle fa' ;
And up there raise an erlish cry,
   ' He's won among us a' ! ' "

   *-Minstrelsy of the Scottish Border*, II. 201.


### PAGE 82, LINE 1.

#### *Merlin Sylvestris.*

The name of Merlin, poet, seer, and wizard, is a
familiar one in the upper part of the Valley of the

Tweed. He is said to have wandered during the latter part of his life, among the wilds of Drummelzier and Tweedsmuir, then covered with birch and hazel, and the centre of the Coed Celyddon, or Wood of Caledon. Nemus Caledonis. He met his death, according to tradition, at the hands of the shepherds of Meldred, a regulus or princeling of the district. Merlin is a somewhat shadowy historical figure, but there can be no doubt that at least one person of this name lived somewhere about the middle of the sixth century; and that he died by the Tweed in the district of Drummelzier, which then formed nearly the centre of the Cymric, or British, kingdom of Cumbria. The great and apparently decisive battle of Arderydd between the Christianised and Pagan or Semi-pagan Celts took place in the year 573. Arderydd is supposed to be Arthuret, near Carlisle. Merlin was on the Pagan and losing side, and his master Gwendollew, and his own nephew,—his sister Gwendydd's son,—both fell in the combat. After this defeat, Merlin, in a state of frenzy, fled to the wilds of upper Tweeddale, where he is said to have lived for fifty years. There is every probability that the Tweeddale Merlin, the son of Morvryn, called also Merlin Wylt, Merlin Sylvestris, Merlin Caledonius, was the famous Welsh or Cymric poet of the sixth century. Two poems of Merlin, in Welsh Merddyn, relating to the battle of Arderydd, are to be found in the ancient and famous *Black Book of Carmarthen* (Nos. I. and XVI.). The first is a wail for the loss of the battle. The other is the oldest existing form of the poem, called the *Avallenau*, attributed to Merlin. In this we have some curious glimpses of the bard. We have, besides, the hints out of which sprung subsequent mediæval traditions regarding him, and suggestions of those mythic features ascribed to him in the romances of Brittany. The Avallenau is a series of predictions regarding Cymric history. Seated at the base of an apple-tree at Tal Ardd, in the Wood of Caledon, he sings :—

> " Sweet apple-tree, and a tree of crimson hue,
>   Which grows in concealment in the wood of Celyddon ;
>   Though sought for their fruit, it will be in vain,
>   Until Cadwaladyr comes from the conference of Cadvaon.
>   To the Eagle of Tywi (Teviot) and Teiwi (Tweed) rivers ;
>   And until fierce anguish comes from Aranwynion,
>   And the wild and long-haired ones are made tame."

—Skene's *Four Ancient Books of Wales*, I. 373.

Merlin's friend and master, Taliessin thus refers to him :—

> " And a load that the moon separates,
>   The placid gentleness of Merlin."

Skene's *Four Ancient Books of Wales*, II. 534.

In *Merlin Sylvestris* an attempt has been made to
depict the Merlin of these early poems, and of local
tradition, which may be traced back for many hun-
dreds of years, near, indeed, to his historical time.
In the twelfth century (1150) appeared a Life of
Merlin in Latin verse (*Vita Merlini Caledonii*),
attributed to Geoffrey of Monmouth.  By this time
the mythic element had grown, in great measure,
around the historical character.  Geoffrey refers particularly to the fountain which Merlin frequented, in
these words :—

> " Fons erat in summo cujusdam vertice montis,
>   Undique præcinctus corulis densisque frutetis,
>   Illic Merlinus consederat ; inde per omnes
>   Spectabat sylvas, cursusque, jocosque ferarum."

A spring that wells up amid most beautiful grass and
moss, on the south-west slope of a spur of the great
Broadlaw, where it overlooks the depths of Talla
and the head of Meggat water,—the only fountain on
these wide, bare, solitary uplands,—may well be taken
as the "fons in summo vertice montis," where the seer-
poet sat and soothed his restless spirit, dissatisfied
with the present, and looking longingly into the far
future.

In the *Scotichronicon* of Fordun (L. III., C. 31),
there is an account of the meeting between Merlin—

who belonged, at least in part, to the old Pagan wor-
ship—and Kentigern, the first apostle on Tweedside
of the Christian creed. Merlin is represented, in
accordance with later views, as a Christian, doomed to
penance in the wilds. He is described as follows:—
" Quidam demens, nudus et hirsutus, ab omni solatio
mundiali destitutus, quasi quoddam torvum furiale."
In reply to Kentigern, he says,—" Olim Vortigerni
vates, Merlinus vocitatus, in hac solitudine dira
patiens fata. . . . Eram enim cædis omnium causa
interemptorum, qui interfecti sunt in bello, cunctis in
hac patria constitutis satis noto, quod erat in campo
inter Lidel et Carvanolow situato." For Vortigern I
have ventured to substitute Gwendollew.

PAGE 5, LINE 14.

*Thus one day wandering with his Nimiane.*

" Thei (Merlin and Nimiane) sojourned together
longe time, till it fill on a day that thei went thourgh
the foreste hande in hande, devisinge and disportinge,
and this was in the foreste of Brochelonde, and fonde
a bussh that was feire and high of white hawthorne,
full of floures, and ther thei sat in the shadowe; and
Merlin leide his heed in the damesels lappe, and
she began to taste softly till he fill on slepe; and
II

when she felt that he was on slepe she aroos softly, and made a cerne (circle) with hir wymple all aboute the bussh and all aboute Merlin, and began hir enchantementes soche as Merlin hadde hir taught, and made the cerne IX tymes, and IX tymes hir enchantementes; and after that she wente and satte down by him and leide his heed in hir lappe, and hilde hym ther till he dide awake; and than he looked aboute hym, and hym semed he was in the feirest tour of the worlde, and the most stronge, and fonde hym leide in the feirest place that ever he lay beforn . . . . Ne never after com Merlin oute of that fortresse that she hadde hym in sette; but she wente in and oute whan she wolde."—*Merlin, or the Early History of King Arthur*, a Prose Romance, Part III., 681 (about 1450-1460, A.D.), Early English Text Society.

### PAGE 87. LINE 13.

### *Shaw.*

*Shaw* originally denoted a thicket. This was generally formed of birch and hazel—both natural growths of the Southern valleys and hills. Shaw is also used to designate the brow of a hill, when it rises to a point from a broad base.—This, however.

is a secondary application of the term, and probably arose from this form of hill being usually clothed with indigenous wood.

## PAGE 94. LINE 7.

It was the belief of the people of Cumbria after Camelon, where Arthur fell in 537, that he and his knights were not really dead, but only slept in the halls beneath the triple Eildons by the Tweed, waiting the bugle-call which should restore them to life and action. A stout heart is needed in him who dares to enter the Eildon caverns, and by trumpet-sound break the wizard spell that holds the heroes of the past in their enchanted sleep.

" Woe to the coward that ever he was born,
  Who did not draw the sword before he blew the horn."

*Printed by Robert MacLehose.*

www.ingramcontent.com/pod-product-compliance
Lightning Source LLC
Chambersburg PA
CBHW030620270326
41927CB00007B/1258